HORIZONTAL JESUS

STUDY GUIDE

HORIZONTAL JESUS

STUDY GUIDE

TONY EVANS

HARVEST HOUSE PUBLISHERS
EUGENE, OREGON

HORIZONTAL JESUS STUDY GUIDE

Copyright © 2015 Tony Evans
Published by Harvest House Publishers
Eugene, Oregon 97402
www.harvesthousepublishers.com

ISBN 978-0-7369-6497-5 (pbk.)
ISBN 978-0-7369-6498-2 (eBook)

Printed in the United States of America

15 16 17 18 19 20 21 22 23 / BP-JH / 10 9 8 7 6 5 4 3 2 1

Contents

INTRODUCTION:

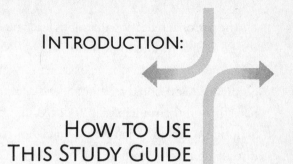

HOW TO USE
THIS STUDY GUIDE

Welcome to the *Horizontal Jesus Study Guide*. It is intended to be used with the book *Horizontal Jesus* to help you go deeper into those truths and apply them to your life. If you are using this study in a small group or at home with your family members, be sure that everyone has access to a copy of the book *Horizontal Jesus* ahead of your start date. Read each chapter in the book before responding to the questions in the corresponding chapter of the study guide.

As you go through the study, you will notice it is divided into various sections:

- subject summary
- personal reflection
- personal application
- questions for journaling or group discussion

Each of these sections has been designed with a unique purpose. The subject summary provides a brief review of the chapter. If you are using this study guide in a group setting, consider reading this section out loud.

The personal reflection questions lead you on a journey through several Scriptures and important thoughts. Keep your Bible handy beside you or on your phone or tablet so you can look up the recommended additional reading. Spend as much time as you need reflecting on the principles introduced in each question and each Scripture you read. Then record your thoughts either in the book directly or in your journal.

The personal application section takes the truths to a more personal and practical level in your life so you can apply them to the decisions you make on a regular basis. These questions will sometimes include additional Scriptures for you to read but will often be focused on how the principles you are learning can best play out in your life. They may call for direct action that you implement later in the week or even that day. Keep a note of your personal challenges and applications so you can track your implementation and progress in these areas of spiritual growth.

Finally, the questions for journaling or group discussion provide thought-provoking prompts for your response. Writing down your thoughts or discussing them with other small-group or family members will help you incorporate the principles you learn into your life. Again, Scriptures are included to provide additional learning opportunities, so keep your Bible handy and be sure to look up and read each verse. If you are in a group situation, everyone's ideas do not have to agree. Allow each person the freedom to express themselves without interruption. In addition, any action steps suggested can be discussed and applied according to your own timetable.

May you enjoy this study and truly experience all God has in store for you as you grow in your vertical relationship with Him and your horizontal relationship with others on His behalf.

1

THE THEOLOGY OF "IT"

Subject Summary

The theology of "it" is based on a principle God established in creation: "The earth brought forth vegetation, plants yielding seed after their kind, and trees bearing fruit with seed in them, after their kind; and God saw that it was good" (Genesis 1:12). Here's how the principle works. All the plants and trees that God created contained seeds so they could reproduce "after their kind." Whatever you plant, that is what you will receive back—after its own kind. You can't plant a pear seed and get watermelons.

This is the way God created life to work. If you want or need something, you first give it away by planting a seed. You take the seed from what you already have in order to replicate it.

Jesus broadened this principle of creation into a principle of life in Luke 6:38. "Give, and it will be given to you. They will pour into your lap a good measure—pressed down, shaken together, and running over. For by your standard of measure it will be measured to you in return."

Whatever you give, that's what you'll get back. God responds to your faith when you give away whatever it is that you need.

To put it another way, if you have a need, make sure you sow that particular kind of seed into other people's lives. Don't just ask God to meet your need without making sure you plant the same kind of seed.

Personal Reflection

1. Why do you think Jesus didn't specify what "it" is in Luke 6:38?

2. Read Psalm 50:10-12 and explain in your own words how this passage supports the statement that God is not a debtor to any human being.

3. How do Psalms 16:2 and 73:25 reinforce the principle that God is to be our only true source for life and everything we need?

4. Second Corinthians 9:6 says, "He who sows sparingly will also reap sparingly, and he who sows bountifully will also reap bountifully." How does this verse reinforce the principle of the seed and Jesus's statement, "By your standard of measure it will be measured to you in return"?

5. Whenever we study a passage of Scripture, we need to take note of the verses preceding and following it. This is important because of the all-too-common practice of lifting a verse out of its context—a dangerous habit that can make the Bible say almost anything the reader wants it to say.

For example, consider a verse that Christians love to quote and memorize: "My God will supply all your needs according to His riches in glory in Christ Jesus" (Philippians 4:19). That's a great promise! Unfortunately, many people quote verse 19 without carefully reading verses 14-18.

You have done well to share with me in my affliction. You yourselves also know, Philippians, that at the first preaching of the gospel, after I left Macedonia, no church shared with me in the matter of giving and receiving but you alone; for even in Thessalonica you sent a gift more than once for my needs. Not that I seek the gift itself, but I seek for the profit which increases to your account. But I have received everything in full and have an abundance; I am amply supplied, having received from Epaphroditus what you have sent, a fragrant aroma, an acceptable sacrifice, well-pleasing to God.

What do you notice about the context in which Paul says God will abundantly meet our needs? (Hint: The Philippian believers planted a seed in Paul's life.) It's also worth noting that the church in Philippi was one of the churches in the region of Macedonia, which Paul described as being in deep poverty.

6. Read 2 Corinthians 8:1-6. What stands out to you about the Philippians' attitude toward giving to advance God's work through the apostle Paul?

Personal Application

1. As we respond to the truths we have learned in this chapter, note the importance of holding our possessions and even the people we love in an open hand. We cannot expect God's blessing if we are interested only in our own benefit. We cannot reap a harvest unless we plant a seed by investing what

He has given us. Our motivation is to further His glory and His kingdom and to be a channel of His blessing others.

Here's an exercise that will help you know whether you are gripping something in your life too tightly. Jot down on a piece of paper what you consider to be your three most valuable possessions. Now ask yourself what would happen if God took one or more of them away. Of course, this may never happen, and nothing is wrong with praying that it won't. But if God did take something from your list, would you be angry with Him? Would your loss shake your faith, or does God have permission to give and take away as He sees fit? To help you visualize your commitment to the Lord, lay your piece of paper in your open hand and give these things to the Lord.

2. Here's a follow-up to the exercise above. Christian stewardship is certainly a key issue for any believer. God will hold us accountable for what He has given us (1 Corinthians 4:2). Are you a good steward of the resources God has entrusted to you? In other words, where and how are you planting seeds that God can bless? It's always a good exercise to occasionally take inventory in this regard. Are you investing your resources to advance God's kingdom? Do you use your skills and talents to help others? Ask God to help you notice opportunities for ministry. A revised to-do list might help you rechannel your resources in more effective ways.

3. Having a deep sense of our own need helps us remember to thank God for His blessings and make the most of them. That's true for intercession. The Holy Spirit is ready to carry your deepest groanings to the Father, but you must engage

Him in heartfelt prayer. How much do you long to experience the Holy Spirit's ministry of intercession on your behalf? That's how much you will experience it.

4. How do you know you're on the right track to receive God's blessing? Compare your pursuit to the weary working man in Ecclesiastes 4:8. He was working himself to death and depriving himself of all pleasure. Is that a snapshot of you? Don't get caught up in the world's methods of chasing happiness. You don't need to shred your soul and exhaust yourself to enjoy God's true blessings. Instead, discover the power of living out the "one anothers" in Scripture. As you meet other people's needs, God in turn meets yours.

5. When it comes to interpreting the Bible's truth and applying it to our lives, we never have to go it alone. God the Holy Spirit wants to "guide you into all the truth" (John 16:13). He wants you to be not only *under* the teaching of the Word but also *in* the Word. He wants to make His Word burn in your heart, because when that happens and you apply what the Holy Spirit of God is teaching you, you will be changed by the power of His transforming Word. Are you engaging that power?

Questions for Journaling or Group Discussion

1. Read the account of Hannah in 1 Samuel 1. She was a godly Israelite woman who was barren. Shame and disappointment were associated with barrenness in that day. So Hannah prayed, "O LORD of hosts, if You will indeed look on the

affliction of Your maidservant and remember me, and not forget Your maidservant, but will give Your maidservant a son, then I will give him to the LORD all the days of his life" (verse 11). What did Hannah want more than anything? What "seed" did she sow by her vow in this verse? How did God honor her seed-planting faith?

Do you believe the seed principle applies to relationships as well as to other things? In what way?

2. Read the story of Jesus's feeding of the 5000 in John 6:1-13. Discuss how this miracle illustrates the seed principle: When you have a need, sow a seed. Give what you need the most, and God is able to make it come back to you in abundance.

3. Take a look at Andrew's assessment of the situation in this setting (John 6:8-9). The other disciples were thinking the same thing. What does their assessment tell us about the disciples' vision and their view of Jesus's power and authority over circumstances?

4. Read Psalm 1:1-3 and discuss its formula for blessing. Why is it such a good pattern for us today as we seek to live spiritually fulfilling lives and enjoy God's blessing?

5. What kind of mindset must we have to enjoy God's blessings? What is the definition of a true blessing? What is not a true blessing?

6. Jesus used the feeding of the multitude to teach the disciples a few truths about the kingdom. What are some lessons Jesus taught the disciples? How might we apply those lessons to our lives today as we consider the principle of the seed and the theology of "it"? To obtain a few more details for your discussion, read the accounts of this great miracle in Matthew 14 and Mark 6 as well.

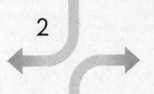

2

THE LAW OF THE HARVEST

Subject Summary

The law of the harvest is explained in 2 Corinthians 9:6-15.

Verse 15 says, "Thanks be to God for His indescribable gift!" Now, if a gift is so good that it can't be described, I want to know about it. So what is this gift that the Bible says is indescribable? We don't have to wonder because the answer is right there in our passage. "God is able to make all grace abound to you, so that always having all sufficiency in everything, you may have an abundance for every good deed" (verse 8).

The gift that God has given to each one of us, the gift that is beyond Paul's ability to articulate, is the gift of grace. Grace is the doctrine that separates Christianity from every other religion ever known to mankind.

Grace operates according to God's laws. In 2 Corinthians 9, grace appears in the context of the law of the harvest, or the law of sowing and reaping. If we are to enjoy the harvest of God's blessings, we need to know how to gain access to His grace. If we don't know what grace is or how to receive it, we won't be able to maximize the gift of grace we have been given.

Accessing the vertical flow of God's grace is no small thing simply because grace is no small thing. In Ephesians 2:7, Paul says God saved us "so that in the ages to come He might show the surpassing riches of His grace in kindness toward us in Christ Jesus." The phrase "the ages to come" is a reference to the endless ages of eternity, which means that God will continue to reveal new aspects of His grace throughout eternity.

But in order to tap into this inexhaustible supply of grace, you have to access it vertically. Let's plug this truth of God's marvelous grace back into our text in 2 Corinthians 9. I'll leave the verse numbers in the quote below because I want you to notice that Paul's statement about grace in verse 8 is sandwiched between verses 6-7 and 9-10, which talk about how to access grace in relationship to the law of the harvest.

> [6]Now this I say, he who sows sparingly will also reap sparingly, and he who sows bountifully will also reap bountifully. [7]Each one must do just as he has purposed in his heart, not grudgingly or under compulsion, for God loves a cheerful giver. [8]And God is able to make all grace abound to you, so that always having all sufficiency in everything, you may have an abundance for every good deed; [9]as it is written, "He scattered abroad, he gave to the poor, His righteousness endures forever." [10]Now He who supplies seed to the sower and bread for food will supply and multiply your seed for sowing and increase the harvest of your righteousness.

These verses relate God's laws about giving and getting to a farming context. I refer to this sowing and reaping as the law of the harvest. If you understand farming, you'll understand how to access God's grace vertically through what you do horizontally.

Personal Reflection

1. The "indescribable gift" discussed in this chapter is often called God's special or saving grace. Another aspect of God's grace is taught in Scripture—Bible teachers refer to it as God's "common" or "general" grace, which He bestows on all of His creatures without exception. Jesus mentions one example of this common grace in Matthew 5:43-45. As you read these verses, note in particular how the latter part of verse 45 illustrates God's common grace to His creation.

2. In 2 Corinthians 8:1-5, Paul gives us an amazing example of a body of believers who not only understood the law of the harvest but also practiced it with joy—despite their meager resources. The churches of Macedonia (verse 1) gave to meet the needs of their fellow saints in Jerusalem despite their own deep poverty (verse 2). Notice five lessons we can learn about giving for the Lord's work:

   • They gave because they understood the incredible gift of God's grace to them.

   • They gave with overflowing, abundant joy.

   • They gave liberally, not simply tossing a few coins in the basket.

   • They gave willingly, without having to be coerced. No one had to beg them. On the contrary, they begged for the privilege of being part of this work.

   • They gave themselves to the Lord first.

3. We need to remember that the law of the harvest works both ways—for blessing and for judgment. According to Galatians

6:7-8, a person reaps whatever he sows. Those who sow to their own flesh will reap the bitter harvest of corruption.

4. When we begin to apply the law of the harvest to our lives, the enemy sometimes whispers in our ear, "Don't be a fool. Look around—a lot of people out there have no regard for God, but they're making it big and don't seem to have any problems. Why should you throw away your hard-earned money when nobody else seems to be doing it?" It's true that as believers, we get upset at times because the wicked people in our world seem to have things their way. If you've ever felt this way, you're in good company. Read Psalm 73 carefully. The psalmist began by lamenting the easy life of the wicked and got himself really worked up about it, falling into the "poor little me" trap. But notice the first word of verse 17—"until." God has the last word in this world, and you belong to Him.

5. God promised His people Israel, "As your days, so shall your strength be" (Deuteronomy 33:25 NKJV). There's a lesson here for us. Often God's provision doesn't arrive until the need arrives. This is a good reminder to avoid running ahead of God. You don't need to lie awake at night worrying about what you are going to eat or drink, or whether you are going to have a roof over your head or clothes to wear tomorrow. Jesus said your Father will supply your needs if you seek first His kingdom and His righteousness (Matthew 6:25-33).

Personal Application

1. In light of the truths we have learned about the law of the harvest, perhaps you're considering taking a step of obedience

in regard to your giving, but you're holding back because you're afraid of what might happen. If so, remember that when we obey God, giving to others in faith for His glory and not for personal gain, we receive the "it" we gave—and often much more.

2. The condition in the previous sentence—sowing for God's glory and not for gain—is absolutely crucial. When people give only so they will receive, they are trying to make a bargain with God. But we can't say to God, "I'll give to Your work but only if You bless my finances." God may want to bless you anyway, but He doesn't do deals. Have you been trying to make any deals with God lately? If so, list a few below. Will you take some time to consider canceling them?

3. The law of the harvest holds true in any area of life where you need to make God-honoring decisions. With this in mind, take a piece of paper and write down the area where you need God's guidance the most right now (whether it's concerning a job, a possible move, a relationship, or whatever). Now ask yourself what God has shown you so far about this issue. Finally, answer these two questions.

- Have I acted on what God has already revealed?
- Am I really ready to take the next step if He were to show it to me today?

4. We've seen the wonderful promise in Philippians 4:19: "My God will supply all your needs according to His riches in Christ Jesus." The phrase "according to" means "in keeping with." In other words, the supply is in character with the God who owns it all.

The preceding 18 verses of Philippians 4 show the context for this promise of a bountiful harvest from God. The Philippians supported Paul—they faithfully gave to God's work. So here's a question to consider. If the Lord were to give you the necessities of life—food, clothing, shelter—"according to" your giving to His work, would you have plenty? Or would you be hungry, naked, and homeless? If you need to change your giving pattern, what specific action step can you take this week?

Questions for Journaling or Group Discussion

1. Why is it important to distinguish between a biblical view of miracles and God's normal way of dealing with His people? What all-too-common misconceptions do many believers have about miracles?

2. Evaluate this statement: "If everything is labeled a miracle, then the biblical concept of miracles comes to mean very little." Do you agree or disagree? Why?

3. A farmer obviously has to sow a seed in order to reap a harvest. The law of the harvest applies in the spiritual realm too. Can you think of an area where you have hoped to reap benefits from God without any sowing at all, or only sowing a little?

4. Do you believe that many people who go to church today have the mentality that God "owes" them a blessing, or that they can "command" Him to bless them? Why might prosperity theology have become so popular?

3

Encouraging One Another

Subject Summary

I often hear people say, "God will not put more on me than I can bear."

Let's debunk that myth right now. In 2 Corinthians 1:8, Paul wrote, "We do not want you to be unaware, brethren, of our affliction...that we were burdened excessively, beyond our strength, so that we despaired even of life."

If ever there was an unbearable situation, Paul was in it. And Paul hadn't done anything to cause it. In fact, he had followed God's leading straight into a place of despair. When we experience similar feelings, we're in good company.

God sometimes allows painful situations in our lives to accomplish His greater purpose for us. He may be directing our focus onto Him. God wants us to learn the power that comes from living in dependence on Him so we can accomplish everything He has for us to do.

Paul reveals this key principle in his next statement. "Indeed, we had the sentence of death within ourselves so that we would not trust in ourselves, but in God who raises the dead...He on whom we have set our hope" (verses 9-10).

In order to take Paul deeper in faith, God put him in a situation in which his résumé, abilities, and connections were of no value. Why? So that Paul would learn to trust God at a deeper level. Hopelessness is a lot like that. Hope comes only through trusting that God is sovereign and that He will empower us to pass through the mess of the past and the chaos of today and enter into a fruitful tomorrow.

Yet when we are facing struggles of this stature, we often can't hope on our own. That's why God asked us to encourage one another. We are to intervene in others' lives to remind them of the truths of God's Word, His promises, and His purposes for pain.

God can touch our mess and make a miracle if we put our hope in Him. He promises, "Those who hopefully wait for Me will not be put to shame" (Isaiah 49:23). God can do more than merely bring us out of our disappointment and despair. He can even cause us to forget how deep it was.

When other people seem to be overwhelmed by hopelessness, you may wonder how they could ever overcome it. But if you will encourage them to do as Abraham did, who believed "in hope against hope" (Romans 4:18), God will honor their trust. He will turn their emotional pain into victorious gain.

Personal Reflection

1. Consider the value of patience. When you own this virtue yourself and experience its benefits, you can encourage others to wait well in their own times of disappointment and despair. Obstacles don't get solved overnight. God often brings us through times of trial and what I call the wilderness in order

to strengthen our faith. Learn how to wait well and encourage others to wait well when problems don't just go away. You wait well by affirming God's faithfulness in your thoughts, words, and actions. You also wait well by spending time with Him in prayer and worship and by showing restraint in complaining, gossiping, whining, and resorting to laziness or overindulgence.

2. Our dependence on anything but Christ leads to instability and hopelessness in the long run. In addition to overcoming our original problem, we now have to overcome an addiction or codependency. Jesus knew we would face the burdens and stresses we do. He knew what happened was going to happen. He saw what was done, and He knows we can be overwhelmed and shrink back in fear and emotional bondage.

   That is why in Matthew 11:28-29, He gave us these compassionate words: "Come to Me, all who are weary and heavy-laden, and I will give you rest. Take My yoke upon you and learn from Me, for I am gentle and humble in heart, and you will find rest for your souls." Memorize these words and let this truth abide in your heart. Then, when friends are struggling with hopelessness, remind them of this verse and encourage them to apply it to their situation.

3. Make two columns on a piece of paper. Now think of a friend or family member who is struggling with disappointment and despair. In one column, write down what this person thinks about the problem, how it makes them act, and the possible outcome. In the other column, write down your own thoughts about this person's situation, your possible actions, and the potential outcome. Notice how thoughts can affect outcomes.

4. Now apply this to something you are struggling with. Write down your thoughts, actions, and possible outcomes. Then write down what someone who does not struggle in this area might think, do, and experience.

Personal Application

1. You can sharpen your own encouragement skills by recognizing what encourages you. In what ways do people lift you up when you are feeling down? Look for opportunities to do these things for others.

2. Everyone likes to be spoken of highly. You can practice the virtue of encouragement by including a positive statement about someone when you introduce him or her to someone else. Try making a habit of this.

3. When you're tempted to ask, "How can I help?" ask instead, "Would it help if I _____?" This is much more helpful because you are actively encouraging others rather than

passively waiting for them to ask for assistance. They may be so discouraged that they don't even know how you can help unless you offer an idea. Also, if they have to come up with the idea, they are likely to feel as if they're imposing on you even though you made yourself available.

4. Have you been with someone who was constantly busy with their phone or some other distraction? Encouragement is more than just words—it's the gift of your full presence. When you are with people who need encouragement, make sure to avoid distractions and give them the gift of your undivided attention.

Questions for Journaling or Group Discussion

1. What things are particularly encouraging to you?

2. Why is it important for each member of the body of Christ to take on this responsibility of encouraging others?

3. What are some ways you can encourage those in your immediate circle? Discuss how you will seek to do this in the next few days.

4. Can you encourage others without providing solutions to their problems? How?

5. In what ways does encouragement combat hopelessness or despair?

6. A gentle touch to the hand, arm, or shoulder is a powerful way to give someone encouragement. How do athletes show encouragement to teammates who muff a play? Why is it important for teammates to do this?

4

LOVING ONE ANOTHER

Subject Summary

People thrive on community. We need each other. Whether for companionship, encouragement, or just plain fun, we enjoy doing things together. In fact, we were created for relationship. That's what makes God's "brand" all the more important. Yes, God has a brand. His identity, logo, and values set Him and His people apart from all others. As members of the body of Christ, we are to manifest His brand in what we say and do so that there is no question who we are and whom we represent.

What is God's brand? It isn't people carrying Bibles underneath their arms. Neither is it "Christianese"—language designed to make some people sound holier or more spiritual than others. It isn't church attendance on Sundays or Wednesdays. No, God's brand is not an external look or activity. Instead, it's ingrained in the very fabric of life.

To know God's brand is to know His heart and His character. To reflect His brand is to reflect Christ Himself. Jesus told us what God's brand is—the one trait we are to be known for—when He gathered His disciples together in the upper room to give them His final message prior to His death and resurrection. In that room, He told them the identifying factor of belonging to Him as His follower.

We read about this in John 13, where Jesus emphasizes the great command to love. Three times in this chapter Jesus tells us we are to love others. Three times He takes us to this all-important principle—His brand. In fact, He comes right out and says that if we love one another, all men will know that we are reflecting Him as His disciples. We are living like a horizontal Jesus to one another.

Personal Reflection

1. All things exist for God's glory. Romans 11:36 says, "From Him and through Him and to Him are all things. To Him be the glory forever. Amen." God's glory is His highest goal. Paul said that everything is *from* God. He is the first cause. Then Paul said that everything is *through* Him. God is also the effective cause of everything in creation. And finally, Paul said that everything is *to* Him. He is the final cause. It all returns to Him to bring Him glory forever.

   God created everything in the universe for His pleasure and His glory (Revelation 4:11). That includes you (Isaiah 43:7). His glory is your chief aim, your highest purpose. You are to reflect Him and His ways through your thoughts, choices, and actions so that when people look at you, they can't help but give glory to God. Read Isaiah 48:11, Acts 7:2, Ephesians 1:6, and 2 Thessalonians 1:9. What do these verses say about God's *intrinsic* glory?

2. Read 1 Chronicles 16:29 and 1 Corinthians 6:20. What do these verses say about God's *ascribed* glory? Compare and contrast God's intrinsic glory and His ascribed glory. Notice the part you play in ascribing glory to an already glorified God.

3. In John 13:31-35, what specific action does Jesus tie to glorifying God? In verse 35, what else do you accomplish in addition to glorifying God when you intentionally love others?

4. Four types of love appear in the Bible—*philos, philostorgos, eros,* and *agape*. Read the following passages and write out what they tell you about love.

   "It was the Mary who anointed the Lord with ointment, and wiped His feet with her hair, whose brother Lazarus was sick. So the sisters sent word to Him, saying, 'Lord, behold, he whom You love is sick'" (John 11:2-3).

"You have heard that it was said, 'You shall love your neighbor and hate your enemy.' But I say to you, love your enemies and pray for those who persecute you" (Matthew 5:43-44).

"May he kiss me with the kisses of his mouth! For your love is better than wine. Your oils have a pleasing fragrance, your name is like purified oil; therefore the maidens love you" (Song of Solomon 1:2-3).

"Be devoted to one another in brotherly love; give preference to one another in honor" (Romans 12:10).

5. The type of love Jesus referred to in John 13:35 is agape. We express agape when we compassionately and righteously pursue the well-being of another. How has the Lord demonstrated this type of love in your own life? How have

others expressed it to you? How is agape different from friendship or romance?

Personal Application

1. First Timothy 1:5 states, "The goal of our instruction is love from a pure heart and a good conscience and a sincere faith." The heart is the spiritual center of who you are. When Paul tells us we are to love from a pure heart, he is stating that the love we give to others must resonate from a place of authenticity within that is untainted by selfishness or sin. Of course, no one is able to love perfectly apart from God Himself, but consider how you might be able to love others without seeking your own benefit. This week, note the things you do and say that show love to someone else. Were you motivated by a pure heart and a desire to see the other person benefit?

2. The opposite of "sincere faith" is "works of the law." In the book of Galatians, Paul taught against a faith based on good works. He was addressing believers who had been saved by grace but then sought to be justified through good works. To love with a "sincere faith" is to love as an act of gratitude, believing that God takes pleasure in what you are doing on His behalf. Consider how this is different from loving others in order to earn God's love and approval through your actions.

What are some actions of love you can do this week that you may not normally be motivated to do? Let your motivation be to express your gratitude and faith in God's love for you.

3. You can do several things to demonstrate that you love someone else, including listening, encouraging, serving, giving a gift, or simply spending time with them. Talk with your close friends or family to discover what things you do for them or with them that make them feel loved. Then take a moment and share with them what they do for you or with you that makes you feel loved.

4. The Bible says, "Do not love the world nor the things in the world. If anyone loves the world, the love of the Father is not in him" (1 John 2:15). Here's a paraphrase of what God may be saying to us: "If you want the world, you can have the world, but you can't have the world and Me. You can love one of us, but you can't love both of us." This agrees with what Jesus said in Luke 16:13 (NIV): "No servant can serve two masters. Either you will hate the one and love the other, or you will be devoted to the one and despise the other. You cannot serve both God and money." To love God and love others, we must make a choice. In what ways does your love for the world or the things in the world negate your love for God or for others?

How can you begin to shift your love from the world or the things in the world to God and others in His name?

Questions for Journaling or Group Discussion

1. Why do you think it is important to distinguish between the four different types of love available to humanity? How is agape set apart from the others?

2. Name and discuss some of the things that make it difficult to love one another. How might self-preservation or self-protection sometimes stand in the way of carrying out this command?

3. What are some visible ways you can love those in your family, small group, church, and community? Choose one to carry out this week.

4. How does loving one another reflect that we are Christ's disciples like nothing else can?

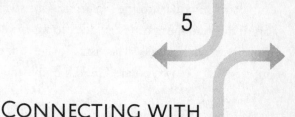

5

Connecting with One Another

Subject Summary

We're living in a day when connection has become a pretty big deal. Now, I'm not computer savvy, but I do know enough to know that the Internet and smartphones have made connecting a priority of everyday life. Computers and tablets and smartphones, Instagram and Pinterest and Twitter...digital media have dominated our connectivity and raised it to another level. All day long, people are communicating with each other through texts, chats, emails, and more. People you know will tag you, and people you don't know hashtag things that interest you. As this happens, our desire for connectivity continues to grow. This is because each of us innately hungers for connection.

We recognize this desire for relationship in our connectivity-crazy culture, but this hunger is not new to twenty-first-century social media. It started with something God had in mind when He created us. This is explained for us in detail in 1 Corinthians 12, which is the most comprehensive statement in the New Testament on the importance of connecting horizontally and vertically. This subject is so critical to the victorious Christian life that the Holy Spirit directed the apostle Paul to commit the entire chapter to the priority of connectivity. The visual image of it can be summarized in verse 27: "Now you are Christ's body, and individually members of it."

When God sets out to give us an illustration of connectivity, He uses something all of us can identify with—a body. Each of us has a physical body. Therefore, each of us knows that the body does what the head tells it to do. If the head says, "Walk," the body walks. If the head says, "Raise your arm," the body raises its arm. In other words, our bodies are completely responsive to our brains.

When your brain says one thing and your body does something else, you need to see a doctor. The job of the physical body is to reflect the dictates of the brain.

Scripture is clear that Jesus Christ is the head of the church, which He calls His body. Therefore, the job of Jesus's body—that's us—is to reflect the dictates of our head, Jesus Christ. To do anything else is dysfunction. To do anything else produces chaos, confusion, and pain. Only when we are properly aligned underneath the goals, visions, and directives of Jesus Christ do we fully function as we were designed.

Personal Reflection

1. Consider what would happen if one of your body parts were disconnected from the rest of your body. Would you be able to tell it what to do? Would it be able to function? What would eventually happen to it?

   Now compare this analogy to the body of Christ. What happens when we are disconnected from one another?

2. In the book *Trust Works! Four Keys to Building Lasting Relationships*, Ken Blanchard, Cynthia Olmstead, and Martha Lawrence lay out seven best practices for connecting with others. Write out one or two ways you are doing each one well and one or two ways you can do each one better.

Listen well.

Praise others' efforts.

Show interest in others.

Share about yourself.

Work well with others.

Ask for input.

Show empathy for others.

3. Research has demonstrated that we perform better and are more satisfied in life when we have meaningful connections. They free us to explore and learn in a safe and secure environment. Without meaningful connections, we are in survival mode and bypass things like ingenuity, creativity, passion, and vision. Meaningful relationships include such characteristics as...

> mutual understanding
> the freedom to love and care and to be loved and cared for
> enjoyment and pleasure
> sharing of stimulating yet diverse ideas
> validation of emotions and value
> help in times of need

Which of these are most important to you? What else would you like to experience in your closest relationships?

Do you have at least a few meaningful relationships in your life? If not, how can you begin to cultivate them? Remember, the best way to gain a friend is to be a friend.

Personal Application

1. Read the following verses and write a reflection on their meaning in your own words.

   "Do not be deceived: 'Bad company corrupts good morals'" (1 Corinthians 15:33).

   "Two are better than one because they have a good return for their labor. For if either of them falls, the one will lift up his companion. But woe to the one who falls when there is not another to lift him up" (Ecclesiastes 4:9-10).

   "Ruth said, 'Do not urge me to leave you or turn back from following you; for where you go, I will go, and where you lodge, I will lodge. Your people shall be my people, and your God, my God'" (Ruth 1:16).

"...not forsaking our own assembling together, as is the habit of some, but encouraging one another; and all the more as you see the day drawing near" (Hebrews 10:25).

2. What can you do this week to connect with someone new or reconnect with someone you haven't spoken with recently? Make an effort to call, write a note, set up a lunch date, or connect in some other way.

3. Do you attend church regularly? If not, consider attending each week to build healthy connections. Are you in a small group or Sunday school class? Discover how these can help you develop meaningful relationships over time.

4. With the onset of texting, email, and social media, many of us are losing the art of verbal communication. List some simple opportunities to add more verbal communication to your life with family members, coworkers, and friends. Then begin to apply these strategies.

Questions for Journaling or Group Discussion

1. Is "connectivity" a major focus of your church? If yes, how? If no, how might your church help build relationships?

2. Why do members in the body of Christ need to be connected to others? In what ways does the whole church benefit when we connect with one another?

3. What are some hindrances to achieving connectivity among members in the body of Christ? Why do we sometimes struggle to build relationships outside of our own church, denomination, culture, or race?

4. What can you do as a small group to enhance your relational connectivity? Discuss these and choose a few to implement as a group.

5. What are some differences between connecting and codependency?

6

ACCEPTING ONE ANOTHER

Subject Summary

One day an elderly woman in worn and tattered clothes visited a local church. At the end of the service, when the preacher invited seekers to come forward, she responded and asked to become a member. She told the preacher she believed in Christ and wanted to be baptized. She also mentioned that she had been cleaning houses all her life.

The preacher thought, "She's so disheveled, and she smells like she's been cleaning toilets. What would the members think of her?" He suggested that she go home and pray about being baptized. The next week, she again came forward during the invitation. She told the preacher she had prayed about it and still wanted to be baptized. But the preacher told her to go home and pray some more.

A few weeks later, the preacher ran across the elderly woman while out doing some errands. He asked why she hadn't been at church for a while. "Is everything all right?" he asked.

"Oh, yes," she said. "I talked with Jesus, and He told me not to worry about becoming a member of your church."

"He did?" said the preacher, a little taken aback.

"That's right," she replied. "Jesus said He's been trying to get into your church for years but hasn't been able to."

Precious few of us ever fully live up to each other's expectations. The story of the cleaning lady is extreme, but we often allow our differences to divide us. Members of the body of Christ have unique backgrounds, preferences, and idiosyncrasies. We can let this diversity bring a greater variety and strength to the body of Christ, or we can let it divide us.

When God brought us together into one big family, He joined together people who have a variety of likes and dislikes, interests, dreams, and baggage. He asked us not only to get along but also to love one another. The apostle Paul wrote, "There is neither Jew nor Greek, there is neither slave nor free man, there is neither male nor female; for you are all one in Christ Jesus" (Galatians 3:28). Yet even though we came from various backgrounds, we are joined together as one new man in Christ (Ephesians 2:15).

Despite our different histories, preferences, and the like, God has asked us to live, work, and worship together in unity as members of the family of God. In order to do that, we have to embrace Paul's admonition to accept one another. Our many rifts reveal that precious few of us have actually put flesh on Paul's words in Romans 15:7: "Therefore, accept one another, just as Christ also accepted us to the glory of God."

We are called as brothers and sisters in Christ to accept one another just as Christ accepted us. Accepting one another is critical if we are to celebrate and enjoy the freedom we have in the Lord.

Personal Reflection

1. Romans 2:11 says, "There is no partiality with God." Where do you tend to show partiality? Make a list of prejudices you

hold, and note whether you feel they are justified. Then pray and ask the Holy Spirit to give you God's heart in these areas.

2. In Luke 6:42 we read, "How can you say to your brother, 'Brother, let me take out the speck that is in your eye,' when you yourself do not see the log that is in your own eye? You hypocrite, first take the log out of your own eye, and then you will see clearly to take out the speck that is in your brother's eye." Can you identify an area in your life that is like a log in your eye? We often see faults in others more easily than in ourselves. Notice where you find fault with others and look to see if you exhibit a similar weakness. Ask God to forgive you in this area and to heal you so He can use you to help others.

3. There is a significant difference between a personal conviction and a personal preference. A personal conviction is something you think is wrong even if the Bible does not come out and specifically say so. For example, if (for some reason) I think that taking a cruise is wrong, then for me to take a cruise would be a sin simply because I was violating my own convictions.

However, when we condemn others for not living according to our personal convictions (that is, issues the Bible does not address), we are judging wrongly. In the chapter, we contrasted judgments and preferences. Write out definitions of both in your own words. How do they apply to you? How do they apply to others?

Personal Application

1. In what areas can you make more room for other people's preferences?

2. Romans 14:13 tells us that we are not to put a stumbling block in anyone's way. Can you identify anything in your life that could cause others to stumble? If you can, take that before the Lord and ask Him to help you remove that hindrance to others' growth.

3. The kingdom of God is righteousness, peace, and joy in the Holy Spirit. That includes accepting each other where we are at and not trying to impose our values or freedoms on others. Is anyone trying to impose their values on you in an area that the Bible doesn't address? How can you prevent their judgment from adversely affecting you?

Questions for Journaling or Group Discussion

1. Look back at each person's definitions of judgment and preference. Discuss these definitions in your group and outline ways to be more accepting of people's preferences that don't violate God's laws.

2. Review and discuss the three principles for acceptance.

   • Do not judge others based on your own personal preferences.

   • Do not be a stumbling block.

   • Do not cause another to violate their conscience.

3. After you have discussed the three principles for acceptance, list one or two more that are based on Scripture and life experience.

4. Identify areas where the body of Christ has failed to distinguish between preferences and God's law. How has this kept the church from impacting the culture for good?

5. What can you do to be more intentional about accepting others from now on?

7

WELCOMING ONE ANOTHER

Subject Summary

In 1 Peter 4:9, the apostle Peter says, "Be hospitable to one another without complaint." Peter envisions the family of God as a hospitable environment where "welcome" is not just a word or a pleasantry, but a way of life. The Greek word translated "be hospitable" means to fondly receive a guest or to graciously welcome a stranger. It's more than saying words, although it involves that. It also includes an action and an attitude. As we'll discover in this chapter, biblical welcoming contains all three—articulation, action, and attitude.

When we practice hospitality as an expression of the Christian life, God blesses others through us. But did you know that when we welcome others, we get blessed too? Here's how.

As human beings born with a sin nature, we are all prone to selfishness. Have you ever noticed that children don't have to be taught how to be selfish? This character defect comes naturally to them and to each of us. We don't have to practice being selfish—we're good at it from day one. And unfortunately, unless we do something about it, we get better and better at it as we grow older.

Many folks don't attend worship *service* on Sundays. Rather, they attend worship *selfish*. They come to be blessed, encouraged, inspired, forgiven, prayed for...with no thought of serving anyone else. Yet Paul tells us, "So then, while we have opportunity, let us do good to all people, and especially to those who are of the household of the faith" (Galatians 6:10). Read that again and notice what it *didn't* say. It didn't say we are to "*receive* good from all people," but rather to "*do* good to all people." The word "do" is an action word, and it clearly underlines the intentionality we are to have as members of the body of Christ to be the hands and feet of Jesus to one another.

This is not a passive call to kindness, but rather an active call to engagement. It means seeking out occasions that God brings your way to warmly welcome others, or to show hospitality to them. As Paul writes, "Let love be without hypocrisy...contributing to the needs of the saints, practicing hospitality" (Romans 12:9,13).

This principle is so important that Paul includes hospitality in his list of qualifications for leaders in the church (1 Timothy 3:2). He also writes that a widow may receive financial assistance only if she has "a reputation for good works; and if she has brought up children, if she has shown hospitality to strangers, if she has washed the saints' feet, if she has assisted those in distress, and if she has devoted herself to every good work" (1 Timothy 5:10).

Hospitality was an expected way of life in first-century Christian culture. People were to open their hearts and demonstrate their attitude by their actions. Christianity was more than a handshake, a pat on the back, and the words, "God bless you." True Christian fellowship is characterized by people serving others and meeting their needs. Sometimes, where appropriate, that includes meeting the needs of people you don't know.

Personal Reflection

1. Search the word "hospitality" online, and you'll find definitions like this: "The friendly and generous reception and entertainment of guests, visitors, or strangers." That leaves it pretty wide open, doesn't it? Hospitality can involve anything that makes others feel welcome. Is this your personal definition of hospitality as well? Have you seen people show hospitality to strangers? What did they do?

2. Write out these Bible verses.

    Hebrews 13:2

    1 Peter 4:9

Romans 12:13

Leviticus 19:34

Titus 1:8

Acts 28:2

3. Commit these verses to memory over the course of the next week and watch how the Holy Spirit brings them to mind when you have opportunities to show hospitality.

4. Are you a hospitable person? How can you improve in this area? How can you mentor someone in this area?

Personal Application

1. The Greek word translated "hospitality" is *philoxenos*, which is a combination of the two root words *philos* (friend or friendship) and *xenos* (stranger). Therefore, *philoxenos* refers to treating strangers as friends. Biblical hospitality is about more than making a meal. It is about demonstrating kindness to someone in need. List some ways to show hospitality besides inviting someone to dinner.

2. How did Martha show hospitality to Jesus and His disciples (Luke 10:38-42)? How did she fail to show hospitality?

3. In the Bible, people showed hospitality by providing...

   a place for spiritual teaching (Romans 16:5)
   encouragement (1 Thessalonians 5:11)
   a meal (Matthew 14:15-21)
   physical safety (2 Kings 4:8-17)
   a place to rest (Mark 6:31)

   Consider how you can provide these things to others.

4. Make a plan for incorporating the art of hospitality in your life. Establish reasonable goals. Consider something simple, such as inviting someone over for tea or allowing a small group to meet in your home, or something larger, such as offering a traveling missionary family a place to stay when they come through your area.

Questions for Journaling or Group Discussion

1. When we consider hospitality, we often think of serving meals to guests in our homes. Hospitality includes this, but it can include so much more. What are some other ways men and women can show hospitality at home, at work, or in the community?

2. Jesus practiced hospitality when He fed 5000 men (plus women and children) who had followed Him into a deserted area. Hospitality doesn't always have to happen at home. What are some creative ways people can practice hospitality outside of the home?

3. How could your church or small group be more hospitable? How can you help?

4. How do you feel when you practice hospitality to someone who appreciates your kindness? How do you feel when you practice hospitality to someone who doesn't show gratitude? How does this impact your desire to practice hospitality?

5. Churches used to meet in homes—and still do in many countries. What are the advantages and disadvantages of having church gatherings in homes? How can typical American churches benefit from this ancient tradition?

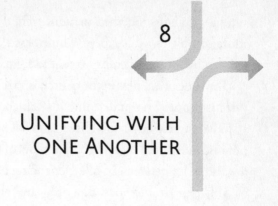

8

UNIFYING WITH ONE ANOTHER

Subject Summary

Unity is not uniformity, nor is it sameness. Just as the Godhead is made up of three distinct Persons—the Father, the Son, and the Holy Spirit—unique in personhood and yet at the same time one in essence, unity reflects oneness *and* individuality. Unity does not mean everyone needs to be like everyone else. God's creativity displays itself in humanity's different shapes, colors, and styles. Each of us is unique. Unity occurs when we combine our unique differences to reach a common goal. It is the sense that the thing that we are gathered for and moving toward is bigger than our own individual preferences.

The church is an earthly reflection of God's heavenly kingdom. He has reconciled racially divided groups into one new man (Ephesians 2:14-15), uniting them into a new body (verse 16) so that the church can function as one. In the church, racial, gender, and class distinctions no longer divide us because of our unity in Christ (Galatians 3:28). This does not negate differences—in fact, unity requires that those differences remain intact and are embraced. Joining our unique strengths together, we add strength to strength, making a more complete and balanced whole based on our mutual relationship with Christ and commitment to Him.

The issue of oneness in the church is so important, we are to look out for people who undermine it (Romans 16:17). God promised to judge those who divide His church (1 Corinthians 3:17). This is because the church is to reflect the values of the kingdom of God to a world in desperate need of experiencing Him.

The church provides the only authentic cross-racial, cross-cultural, and cross-generational basis for oneness. It is the only institution on earth obligated to live under God's authority while enabled to do so through His Spirit.

Personal Reflection

1. Jesus provided a clear warning that division leads to ruin.

> Any kingdom divided against itself is laid waste, and
> any city or house divided against itself will not stand. If
> Satan casts out Satan, he is divided against himself; how
> then will his kingdom stand? (Matthew 12:25-26).

How do personal biases based on class, race, and gender get in the way of advancing God's kingdom agenda in your own life?

2. Do any of your relationships suffer from a lack of unity? What can you do to bring about a spirit of unity in these relationships? How can you build cross-cultural relationships for the benefit of God's kingdom purposes?

3. In what ways might you hold some prejudice against other classes, races, or genders? Consider each example in the light of God's viewpoint on equality.

4. Read and reflect on the following verses and write out a summary statement of each in your own words.

   "To sum up, all of you be harmonious, sympathetic, brotherly, kindhearted, and humble in spirit" (1 Peter 3:8).

"Make my joy complete by being of the same mind, maintaining the same love, united in spirit, intent on one purpose" (Philippians 2:2).

"Beyond all these things put on love, which is the perfect bond of unity" (Colossians 3:14).

"Just as we have many members in one body and all the members do not have the same function, so we, who are many, are one body in Christ, and individually members one of another" (Romans 12:4-5).

"Preserve the unity of the Spirit in the bond of peace" (Ephesians 4:3).

Personal Application

1. In Ephesians 4:3 we are instructed to preserve the unity of the Spirit, not to create it. The Spirit of God has already provided for our unity. The closer we are to God through abiding with Him, the closer we are to preserving unity. What can you do to make sure you are abiding in God this week?

2. Personal preferences and denominational distinctives exist in the body of Christ. We have not been called to conform to each other but rather to unify around a common goal of making Jesus Christ known. What personal preferences tend to repel you from other believers? What differences can you begin to accept in order to work together toward a common goal?

3. Think of one way you can step out of your racial, ethnic, or cultural comfort zone this month. Could you visit a church, volunteer at a school, or take part in a ministry? Find a way to cross at least one dividing line this week.

Questions for Journaling or Group Discussion

1. What was Paul's justification for admonishing Peter in Galatians 2?

2. What does living in unity have to do with spreading the gospel?

3. Read Psalm 133:

> Behold, how good and how pleasant it is
> For brothers to dwell together in unity!
> It is like the precious oil upon the head,
> Coming down upon the beard,
> Even Aaron's beard,
> Coming down upon the edge of his robes.
> It is like the dew of Hermon
> Coming down upon the mountains of Zion;
> For there the LORD commanded the blessing—life
> forever.

This is one of only two places in Scripture where God commands a blessing (the other is Deuteronomy 28:8). What criteria does the psalmist mention for God to command His blessing? What does this imply about the call to unity?

4. One of the greatest reasons God calls us to unity is so that we will be a testimony to the world of the sacrifice of Jesus Christ and the love of God the Father. Through unity we are able to live our lives as a horizontal Jesus to those who do not yet know Him. Jesus prayed,

> I do not ask on behalf of these alone, but for those also who believe in Me through their word; that they may all be one; even as You, Father, are in Me and I in You, that they also may be in Us, so that the world may believe that You sent Me (John 17:20-21).

How does unity encourage the world to believe that God sent Jesus Christ? How is God's glory manifested in unity (verses 22-23)?

5. What examples of the power of unity do we see in the world? (Think of athletic teams, lobbyists, special-interest groups…) How often do we witness that same power in causes based on God's kingdom agenda? What can we do to increase our influence and transform our culture for good?

9

SERVING ONE ANOTHER

Subject Summary

People who love old westerns remember the *The Hanging Tree*. "Doc" Frail (Gary Cooper) finds Rune (Ben Piazza), a young man who's been shot and is dying. Doc removes the bullet and saves Rune's life. When Rune asks what he can do to show his gratitude, Doc says something to this effect: "I've always needed an assistant, so why don't you assist me? I'll teach you what to do." When Rune asks how long the doctor wanted his help, Doc replies, "For the rest of your life. That's how long you would have been dead if I hadn't saved you."

God has said to you and me this is what He wants. For the rest of your life on earth, since He saved you, He wants you to yield yourself to His purposes, His pleasure, and His goals by serving Him. One way you serve God is by serving others.

In Mark 9:34, we find the disciples arguing about who was the greatest. Jesus's response sheds light on the high value of servanthood. This isn't a value that most of us live out in our daily lives. The world doesn't esteem it. However, in God's economy, service is one of the most prestigious things you can do.

"Do you want to be great?" Jesus said, in essence. "Great! Then serve, and you will be."

Service is the true path to significance. Service to others horizontally opens up your engagement with God vertically because when you serve, He recognizes kingdom greatness in you. If you want to have a more powerful, life-changing vertical experience with God, your horizontal relationships must be characterized by a servant's heart.

Your kitchen appliances don't serve themselves. Toasters don't eat their own toast. Refrigerators don't drink the milk they cool. Stoves don't eat the meat they cook. Appliances are there to serve people. We benefit from them.

God has assigned you a divine purpose, and when you fulfill it, you will benefit others. Carrying out your calling is one way of contributing to the well-being of others and bringing glory to God.

Personal Reflection

1. Do you think of yourself as a servant? What opportunities do you have to serve others? List five acts of service you recall doing recently.

2. Read the following verses. Write down one way you can apply each verse to your own life.

"The Son of Man did not come to be served, but to serve, and to give His life a ransom for many" (Mark 10:45).

"Have this attitude in yourselves which was also in Christ Jesus, who, although He existed in the form of God, did not regard equality with God a thing to be grasped, but emptied Himself, taking the form of a bond-servant, and being made in the likeness of men" (Philippians 2:5-7).

"We do not preach ourselves but Christ Jesus as Lord, and ourselves as your bond-servants for Jesus' sake" (2 Corinthians 4:5).

"Sitting down, He called the twelve and said to them, 'If anyone wants to be first, he shall be last of all and servant of all'" (Mark 9:35).

"You were called to freedom, brethren; only do not turn your freedom into an opportunity for the flesh, but through love serve one another" (Galatians 5:13).

"Whatever you do, do your work heartily, as for the Lord rather than for men, knowing that from the Lord you will receive the reward of the inheritance. It is the Lord Christ whom you serve" (Colossians 3:23-24).

3. Think about how you feel before and after you serve someone. Does their response to your service affect your motivation to do it again? Should it?

Personal Application

1. Name one way you can increase your level of service in each of these areas: at home, at work, at church, and in your community. Seek to implement these acts of service on a regular basis.

2. How do you respond when someone serves you? Are you dismissive? Grateful? Do you try to prevent others from serving you? When others serve you, how important is your response to them and to God? When people who serve you feel valued, they are encouraged in their walk with the Lord. Whom can you thank today for their service?

3. Is it wrong to want to be great? Read Mark 10:35-45 and note Jesus's response to the disciples' desire to be great. Did Jesus correct that desire? Did He tell them it was wrong?

4. What is a biblical definition of greatness?

Questions for Journaling or Group Discussion

1. You can serve a local community by mentoring local students, helping younger students to read, assisting with meals, doing home repairs for the elderly, visiting the sick and elderly…the possibilities are endless. What habits of community service are right for you?

2. Discuss your definitions of greatness. If you are journaling, expand on this concept of biblical greatness. You may also want to read chapter 3 of the book *Kingdom Man*, which delves deeper into the idea of biblically based greatness.

3. Look at the various roles people fill in your local church. Do those who serve behind the scenes receive the appreciation they should? If not, how can you help correct this imbalance?

4. When is it okay *not* to serve?

5. Name some biblical examples of servants and serving.

10

FORGIVING ONE ANOTHER

Subject Summary

When someone sins against you or you commit sins you regret, your soul is wounded. If that wound is left untreated, the sore will fester and the pain will increase. If someone accidentally brushes up against your wound, you'll recoil in pain and lash out at them.

To experience victory through forgiveness, make sure to treat your wounds. Let them heal, and rather than focusing on the scars of your past, focus on your new start. In the context of the "one anothers," we are not only to forgive others but also to help others experience the freedom that comes from forgiveness. We are to remind each other how important it is to let go of past pains and hurts and embrace the promise of each day.

Forgiving others or ourselves can be difficult. Admitting that we are having a hard time forgiving God—that can be even tougher.

Of course, this doesn't mean God has done anything wrong. We are not forgiving Him for sins He has committed, because He does not sin. In fact, just the opposite—we "forgive" Him by not attributing any wrongdoing to Him. We affirm that He is good and has our best interests in mind even when He sovereignly allows us to be wounded.

God was good even when He allowed the devil to test Job with catastrophe after catastrophe. He was good even when He told Ezekiel He was going to take away his wife the very next day. He was good even when He gave Paul a thorn in the flesh. David, the man after God's own heart, speaks regularly about the wounds God had given Him.

In God's sovereignty, He knows the purpose for the pain. He understands the end from the beginning. But from our limited perspective, we often only see the wounds. And it's okay to admit—just as I'll admit—that our wounds can make us angry at God. That may not sound very spiritual, but it's best to acknowledge the truth.

The foundational principle for forgiving God, or for letting go of bitterness and anger when He allows us to experience pain, comes from Romans 8:28. In embracing the truth that all things really do work together for good when you love God and are called according to His purpose, you receive strength and wisdom to view life's trials, disappointments, and pain through the lens of God's good intentions.

Personal Reflection

1. Unforgiveness often keeps us from moving forward. Jesus talked about faith that can move a mountain (Mark 11:22-24), but then He explained why our prayers may not be moving much of anything at all. In the next few verses we read, "Whenever you stand praying, forgive, if you have anything against anyone, so that your Father who is in heaven will also forgive you your transgressions. But if you do not forgive, neither will your Father who is in heaven forgive your transgressions."

Reflect on two dreams or ambitions you've had, even if you have given up on them. They could seem impossible, like moving a mountain. But write them down and remember them as you walk through this process of forgiveness. These are your goals. Letting go of unforgiveness can help you reach them.

2. Can you think of someone you haven't forgiven? If so, can you identify ways that your unforgiveness has spilled over into your interactions with other people?

3. Do you need to forgive yourself for something? Ask God right now to help you think about yourself the way He thinks about you—forgiven and not condemned. Experience the freedom that comes from forgiving yourself.

4. In one 24-hour period, make a note of each time you think about or mention the past. How much of your time is spent living in the past? What steps might help you to seize today and embrace a brighter tomorrow?

5. Give yourself grace. Be patient. Forgiveness is a process of changing your thoughts about a traumatic event. It takes time to consistently implement your decision to forgive (to break free from triggers), and it takes even more time for your emotions to catch up to your decision. Take forgiveness one step at a time. When you feel as if you have failed or regressed, remind yourself, "Forgiveness is a process, and I will get there."

Personal Application

1. Name one person you need to forgive. Every day this next week, pray a simple prayer that God will bless this person. Feel free to add more people to this list if you want.

2. Make two columns on a sheet of paper. In the first column, list a few of your painful personal experiences. In the second column, note how God used each experience for good.

3. List some people or events God has allowed in your life to deepen your relationship with Him and help you grow in spiritual maturity. Thank Him for using each one to help you to become more like Him.

4. Choose an action that will help you release the pain associated with unpleasant memories. You could write them on a piece of paper, tie them to a helium balloon, and let them float away. You could take them to church and leave them at the altar. You could gather some stones, associate each event or person with a stone, and then drop the stones into a lake or river. How will you symbolize your willingness to let go?

Questions for Journaling or Group Discussion

1. What are some of the obstacles to forgiveness? How do they hinder your ability to forgive? How can you overcome them?

2. Have you ever been reluctant to forgive someone because you felt they had not paid for what they had done to you? Did you decide to forgive anyway? If so, how did your forgiveness affect you? How did it affect the other person?

3. List a few times when you have forgiven others. Is forgiveness becoming easier or more difficult for you?

4. Why is it important to remember God's forgiveness of you when considering forgiving someone else?

5. When is it okay *not* to forgive?

6. What are some side effects of *not* forgiving? How does forgiving others affect you?

11

Admonishing One Another

Subject Summary

The apostle Paul expected believers to admonish each other.

> Now may the God of hope fill you with all joy and peace in believing, so that you will abound in hope by the power of the Holy Spirit.
>
> And concerning you, my brethren, I myself also am convinced that you yourselves are full of goodness, filled with all knowledge and able also to *admonish one another* (Romans 15:13-14).

The Greek word translated "admonish" is *noutheteo* (counsel, advise, steer, or warn). Paul uses the same word when he writes, "Let the word of Christ richly dwell within you, with all wisdom teaching and *admonishing* one another with psalms and hymns and spiritual songs, singing with thankfulness in your hearts to God" (Colossians 3:16).

When you and I read that we are to admonish one another, we are being encouraged to counsel, guide, steer, and direct the people in our sphere of influence. The verse isn't saying that we are to be professional psychologists or analysts, but that as Christians in the family of God, we are to provide biblical, spiritual counsel to one another. We are to provide instruction, exhortation, or even warning, depending on the situation, to those who need direction in their lives.

Noutheteo specifically has to do with providing corrective or intentional guidance in order to prevent something that could go wrong or to direct toward something that would be right. It includes guidance away from choices that are sinful as well as those that might simply be unwise. To admonish is to counsel, whether formally or informally.

Paul identifies the goal of our admonishment. "We proclaim Him, *admonishing* every man and teaching every man with all wisdom, so that we may present every man complete in Christ" (Colossians 1:28). The goal of admonishing one another is spiritual maturity. Our aim is to help every man and woman to be complete in Christ, mature and whole. We do this by helping each other build on the solid foundation of biblical truth and wisdom.

Admonishment isn't running around pointing fingers and making people look bad. Rather, it is constructive counsel, guidance, and teaching. As members of Christ's body, we are called to enhance, develop, and invest in one another's spiritual growth. That's not simply the pastor's job or the small-group facilitator's job. That responsibility rests on all of our shoulders. We are to be a horizontal Jesus to one another, offering wisdom, insight, and counsel where needed.

Personal Reflection

1. If our goal is to become a mature Christian and to encourage others to press on to maturity, how do we measure that goal?

What does a mature Christian look like, act like, and sound like? Write out your definition of a mature believer and then read this definition from the chapter.

Mature believers consistently make decisions based on a biblical worldview. They seek to live life under God and His comprehensive rule over everything.

2. Why is it essential that admonition come only from a mature believer? What can happen when admonition comes from an immature believer?

3. Have you ever been admonished by an immature believer? If so, what was the result? Did the admonishment affect your relationship, and if so, how? Did it impact the situation you were being admonished about?

4. In the chapter, spiritual growth is defined as "an ongoing process of development that includes aligning our minds to God's perspective." What are some specific things you can do to grow spiritually? List them and then seek to apply these to your own life.

Personal Application

1. The apostle Paul describes a scenario that could have come from the twenty-first century.

> There are many rebellious men, empty talkers and deceivers, especially those of the circumcision, who must be silenced because they are upsetting whole families, teaching things they should not teach for the sake of sordid gain. One of themselves, a prophet of their own, said, "Cretans are always liars, evil beasts, lazy gluttons." This testimony is true. For this reason reprove them severely so that they may be sound in the faith (Titus 1:10-13).

> What are some common ways we might twist the truth for our own personal gain? For example, have you ever rationalized inappropriate behavior? Blamed others? Focused on outward performance rather than inward motivation?

2. Some people in your church, circle, class, or small group are making unwise choices—even sinful ones. Sermons aren't always going to reach them. Neither will nice songs sung on Sunday morning. What they need is the Holy Spirit showing up in their lives through someone who cares enough to offer heartfelt counsel based on the Word of God. They need a friend. A friend is someone who gets in your way when you are on your way down. That's a true friend. A friend is not someone who rats on you publicly, but someone who tries to restore you privately.

   Have you ever addressed sin in another person's life? Did you do it publicly or privately? Is there anything you could do differently next time to be a more effective horizontal Jesus?

3. Who in your social circle could benefit from a friendly admonishment? Are you spiritually equipped to offer this admonishment gently, humbly, and privately?

Questions for Journaling or Group Discussion

1. What is the difference between biblical admonishment and judgment?

2. What is the difference between biblical admonishment and church discipline?

3. Should church discipline still occur today? If so, who should conduct it and how?

4. Role-play a biblical approach to admonishment. Take several turns and discuss what was positive and negative in each.

5. Is admonishment common in modern-day churches? In your local body of believers? In your circle of friends? If not, how can you create an environment where people can benefit from gracious, loving admonishment?

12

Restoring One Another

Subject Summary

Hospitals exist because people get sick. When people need their health restored, hospitals are there to combat the illness and facilitate healing. At a hospital, doctors and nurses do for others what people cannot do for themselves. They make people well again.

The church, the body of Christ, is God's hospital. One of the primary reasons the church exists is to be a community where people's spiritual lives can be restored. They certainly can't restore themselves. People desperately need help—something has gone wrong in their lives, and the church is there to facilitate healing. As members of God's family, we join together to offer the hope of healing by God's grace. The church family is to be a place where those who are spiritually weak or sick can find help, hope, healing, and restoration in Christ's name.

> Brethren, even if anyone is caught in any trespass, you who are spiritual, restore such a one in a spirit of gentleness; each one looking to yourself, so that you too will not be tempted. Bear one another's burdens, and thereby fulfill the law of Christ (Galatians 6:1-2).

The Greek word translated "restore" means to mend something that has been broken. It sometimes referred to mending a broken bone. The bone would be reset so it could grow back together and be restored to its original function. Or if a fisherman tore his net, he would restore it by mending the place that was torn.

Before people can be restored, they must acknowledge that something has been broken or torn and needs to be mended. In the same way that people go to the hospital to regain their health, people who come to church ought to be able to find restoration for their broken lives. God uses us to mend one another according to our original design as much as possible.

Restoration must happen in the body of Christ, but Paul states clearly that it must be done by the qualified—those who are spiritual. If it is not done "in a spirit of gentleness" and wisdom, the one who is seeking to restore can cause more harm than good and also be pulled into the bondage themselves.

Personal Reflection

1. After King Solomon dedicated the first temple in Jerusalem, the Lord appeared to him with a promise that we often use today when praying for national restoration.

> The Lord appeared to Solomon at night and said to him, "I have heard your prayer and have chosen this place for Myself as a house of sacrifice. If I shut up the heavens so that there is no rain, or if I command the locust to devour the land, or if I send pestilence among My people, and My people who are called by My name humble themselves and pray and seek My face and turn from their wicked ways, then I will hear from heaven, will forgive their sin and will heal their land. Now My

eyes will be open and My ears attentive to the prayer offered in this place. For now I have chosen and consecrated this house that My name may be there forever, and My eyes and My heart will be there perpetually" (2 Chronicles 7:12-16).

2. Consider these four concepts from this passage. How can you apply each one to the process of restoration?

humility

prayer

fellowship with God

turning from sin

3. Is there an area in your life where you need to be restored? Who might be willing and able to walk you through this process?

4. Is there an area in your life where you have experienced restoration? Who can you help in their struggle with a similar issue?

Personal Application

1. Being spiritual has nothing to do with the degrees on your wall or how much education you have. A high school dropout can be more spiritual than a person with a master's degree in theology. And spirituality has nothing to do with how old you are. A person could be 90 years old but have lived carnally for those 90 years.

   What does being spiritual mean to you? How are you pursuing growth in this area?

2. What is biblical spirituality? Can you think of any Scripture verses to support your answer?

3. What is the difference between bearing someone's burden and carrying their load? Have you ever enabled someone by carrying a load they should have carried themselves? What happened?

4. Have you ever borne someone's burden for a short time until they were able to carry their own load? What happened?

5. Who in your small group or circle of friends and acquaintances needs restoration? Has anyone reached out, or is it possible for you to do so? What steps can you take to help restore this person?

Questions for Journaling or Group Discussion

1. What are some things that keep people from restoring each other?

2. What are some common ways that people do more harm than good when trying to restore others?

3. What is the difference between bearing a burden and carrying a load?

4. When should you ask others to assist you as you attempt to restore someone?

5. When a person is in the process of being restored, what fruits should they exhibit?

13

Comforting One Another

Subject Summary

We commonly express our sorrow through tears. Tears are indicative of pain in our lives. They express what we're feeling deeply inside, revealing that something is terribly wrong and that it hurts.

In John 11, Mary is weeping because her dearly loved brother, Lazarus, has died. To make matters worse, her dear friend Jesus, who could have saved Lazarus, didn't come to help when He heard Lazarus was sick. Mary can't hide her sadness—Lazarus is gone, and Jesus seems to have betrayed her. She is so hurt that when she finally does see Jesus, she blames Him for Lazarus's death.

Jesus's response to Mary and the other mourners gives us great insight into the importance of authentic emotion during times of comfort.

> When Jesus therefore saw her weeping, and the Jews who came with her also weeping, He was deeply moved in spirit and was troubled, and said, "Where have you laid him?" They said to Him, "Lord, come and see." Jesus wept (John 11:33-35).

Jesus didn't offer Mary a sermon on the importance of letting go. He didn't scold her for allowing her jumbled emotions to spill out in words of blame and anger. When Jesus saw the pain in those around Him, He was moved in His spirit, and He was so troubled that He wept too.

Why did God weep? After all, wouldn't Christ, the God-Man, know that death is just a passageway into eternity? Couldn't He have sat back and said casually, "Hey, it's going to be okay"? Jesus wept even though He knew all this and more because He saw their pain. He empathized with their hurt. He felt their loss.

As you and I seek to be a horizontal Jesus, we will meet people whose paths are littered with pain and loss. Our first task is to care. We do this by recognizing that people's pain is real even if it isn't always rational. Pain is pain and needs comfort. The worst thing you can do for someone in pain is to tell them there's no reason to be sad. Rather, become like Jesus, who wept with those who wept even though He knew Lazarus would live again. In His weeping, He brought comfort at just the right time—when it was needed most.

Personal Reflection

1. Psychologists often listen to clients for extended periods of time as a way of giving comfort. People often feel a need to tell someone what happened and how they feel. You too can comfort others by offering a listening ear. Reflect on the following traits of a good listener and make a note of any ways you need to improve your skills.

   - makes sustained eye contact
   - offers positive and attentive facial expressions

- does not change the subject
- does not shift the subject to themselves
- uses the 80/20 rule (Spend 80 percent of the time listening and 20 percent of the time offering feedback to what you hear.)
- asks good questions to encourage further thought and verbal processing

2. Have you ever been in a crisis and heard someone say, "I know how you feel"? Chances are they really didn't know how you felt, and you probably picked up on that quickly. Be careful not to toss out that statement when comforting others. Instead, you might say, "How did that make you feel?" or "I may not know exactly how you feel, but I can hear your struggle and pain."

3. How do you feel around someone who is crying?

A study by Dr. William H. Frey II (a biochemist from St. Paul–Ramsey Medical Center in Minnesota) revealed a critical chemical difference between tears produced by stress, tears produced by emotional pain, and tears produced by irritants in the air, such as dust. The study concluded that the tears produced by emotional pain contained a higher level of the protein-based hormones prolactin and leucine enkephalin (a natural pain reducer) as well as other hormones designed to comfort us physically. This is why a person will often feel better following a good cry.

Knowing this, in what ways can you allow yourself to cry more when you need to? Consider being more open to others crying in your presence rather than trying to solve the situation and dry their tears.

4. Here are some practical ways you can comfort someone. Which of these do you do naturally? Which ones can you begin practicing when you comfort others?

- Garner support for the person from others.
- Be willing to listen to the same story again and again.
- Remind and encourage the person to do basic functioning behaviors.
- Call or text in the evening to check on the person. Nighttime is the most difficult for people in pain.
- Include helpful phrases in your conversations and text messages: "This too shall pass." "Hang in there—it will get better."
- Don't pull out too soon. Stay in for the long haul of healing.

Personal Application

1. Do you consider yourself to be a good comforter? If you aren't, in what ways can you improve? If you are, who could benefit from your comfort?

2. Empathy is the ability to understand and share other people's feelings. This differs from sympathy—feelings of pity and sorrow for someone else's misfortune. Do you tend to show empathy or sympathy toward people who are going through trials? Why is empathy a more comforting approach? How can you develop empathy and not just sympathy?

3. When you need to be comforted, do you feel as if others are there for you? If not, what can you do to make sure some people will be available when you need them?

4. In John 11, Jesus comforted Martha and Mary. How did He meet their emotional needs? How did He meet their practical needs?

Questions for Journaling or Group Discussion

1. Here are some ways you can comfort yourself. Write down the name of someone who could benefit from these ideas. How will you share them with this person?

> stretching
> breathing deeply
> listening to comforting music
> walking
> visualizing a positive image
> allowing yourself to feel sad
> talking to others

2. Read the following Bible verses on comfort and note a practical application of each one.

> "Be anxious for nothing, but in everything by prayer

and supplication with thanksgiving let your requests be made known to God" (Philippians 4:6).

"He sets on high those who are lowly, and those who mourn are lifted to safety" (Job 5:11).

"God causes all things to work together for good to those who love God, to those who are called according to His purpose" (Romans 8:28).

"I would have despaired unless I had believed that I would see the goodness of the LORD in the land of the living. Wait for the LORD; be strong and let your heart take courage; yes, wait for the LORD" (Psalm 27:13-14).

"These things I have spoken to you, so that in Me you may have peace. In the world you have tribulation, but take courage; I have overcome the world" (John 16:33).

"Do not fear, for I am with you; do not anxiously look about you, for I am your God. I will strengthen you, surely I will help you, surely I will uphold you with My righteous right hand" (Isaiah 41:10).

"Blessed be the God and Father of our Lord Jesus Christ, the Father of mercies and God of all comfort, who comforts us in all our affliction so that we will be able to comfort those who are in any affliction with the comfort with which we ourselves are comforted by God" (2 Corinthians 1:3-4).

"But in all these things we overwhelmingly conquer
through Him who loved us. For I am convinced that
neither death, nor life, nor angels, nor principalities,
nor things present, nor things to come, nor powers, nor
height, nor depth, nor any other created thing, will be
able to separate us from the love of God, which is in
Christ Jesus our Lord" (Romans 8:37-39).

"Now may the God of hope fill you with all joy and
peace in believing, so that you will abound in hope by
the power of the Holy Spirit" (Romans 15:13).

3. Do you know someone who needs to be comforted? How can
you help?

4. How have you seen believers comfort others and thus express the love of God?

5. When we comfort others, those outside the body of Christ see God's love at work. Have you ever seen this happen? If so, how?

"ONE ANOTHERS" IN SCRIPTURE

Salt is good; but if the salt becomes unsalty, with what will you make it salty again? Have salt in yourselves, and be at peace with one another (Mark 9:50).

If I then, the Lord and the Teacher, washed your feet, you also ought to wash one another's feet (John 13:14).

A new commandment I give to you, that you love one another, even as I have loved you, that you also love one another. By this all men will know that you are My disciples, if you have love for one another (John 13:34-35).

This is My commandment, that you love one another, just as I have loved you (John 15:12).

This I command you, that you love one another (John 15:17).

Be devoted to one another in brotherly love; give preference to one another in honor (Romans 12:10).

Be of the same mind toward one another; do not be haughty in mind, but associate with the lowly. Do not be wise in your own estimation (Romans 12:16).

Owe nothing to anyone except to love one another; for he who loves his neighbor has fulfilled the law (Romans 13:8).

Let us not judge one another anymore, but rather determine this—not to put an obstacle or a stumbling block in a brother's way (Romans 14:13).

Accept one another, just as Christ also accepted us to the glory of God (Romans 15:7).

Concerning you, my brethren, I myself also am convinced that you yourselves are full of goodness, filled with all knowledge and able also to admonish one another (Romans 15:14).

Greet one another with a holy kiss (Romans 16:16; 1 Corinthians 16:20; 2 Corinthians 13:12).

So then, my brethren, when you come together to eat, wait for one another (1 Corinthians 11:33).

God has so composed the body...so that there may be no division in the body, but that the members may have the same care for one another (1 Corinthians 12:24-25).

For you were called to freedom, brethren; only do not

turn your freedom into an opportunity for the flesh, but through love serve one another (Galatians 5:13).

Bear one another's burdens, and thereby fulfill the law of Christ (Galatians 6:2).

Walk in a manner worthy of the calling with which you have been called, with all humility and gentleness, with patience, showing tolerance for one another in love (Ephesians 4:1-2).

Be kind to one another, tender-hearted, forgiving each other, just as God in Christ also has forgiven you (Ephesians 4:32).

Be filled with the Spirit, speaking to one another in psalms and hymns and spiritual songs, singing and making melody with your heart to the Lord (Ephesians 5:18-19).

Be subject to one another in the fear of Christ (Ephesians 5:21).

Do nothing from selfishness or empty conceit, but with humility of mind regard one another as more important than yourselves (Philippians 2:3).

Do not lie to one another, since you laid aside the old self with its evil practices (Colossians 3:9).

Put on a heart of compassion, kindness, humility,

gentleness and patience; bearing with one another, and forgiving each other (Colossians 3:12-13).

Let the word of Christ richly dwell within you, with all wisdom teaching and admonishing one another with psalms and hymns and spiritual songs, singing with thankfulness in your hearts to God (Colossians 3:16).

May the Lord cause you to increase and abound in love for one another, and for all people, just as we also do for you (1 Thessalonians 3:12).

Now as to the love of the brethren, you have no need for anyone to write to you, for you yourselves are taught by God to love one another (1 Thessalonians 4:9).

Comfort one another with these words (1 Thessalonians 4:18).

Encourage one another and build up one another, just as you also are doing (1 Thessalonians 5:11).

Encourage one another day after day, as long as it is still called "Today," so that none of you will be hardened by the deceitfulness of sin (Hebrews 3:13).

Let us consider how to stimulate one another to love and good deeds, not forsaking our own assembling together, as is the habit of some, but encouraging one another; and all the more as you see the day drawing near (Hebrews 10:24-25).

Do not speak against one another, brethren (James 4:11).

Do not complain, brethren, against one another, so that you yourselves may not be judged; behold, the Judge is standing right at the door (James 5:9).

Confess your sins to one another, and pray for one another so that you may be healed. The effective prayer of a righteous man can accomplish much (James 5:16).

Above all, keep fervent in your love for one another, because love covers a multitude of sins. Be hospitable to one another without complaint. As each one has received a special gift, employ it in serving one another as good stewards of the manifold grace of God (1 Peter 4:8-10).

Clothe yourselves with humility toward one another, for God is opposed to the proud, but gives grace to the humble (1 Peter 5:5).

This is the message which you have heard from the beginning, that we should love one another (1 John 3:11).

This is His commandment, that we believe in the name of His Son Jesus Christ, and love one another, just as He commanded us (1 John 3:23).

Beloved, let us love one another, for love is from God;

and everyone who loves is born of God and knows God (1 John 4:7).

Beloved, if God so loved us, we also ought to love one another. No one has seen God at any time; if we love one another, God abides in us, and His love is perfected in us (1 John 4:11-12).

Now I ask you, lady, not as though I were writing to you a new commandment, but the one which we have had from the beginning, that we love one another (2 John 5).

APPENDIX 2

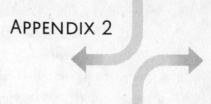

SMALL-GROUP
LEADER'S GUIDE

This material is adapted from the Oak Cliff Bible Fellowship Small Group Leaders Handbook. If you have not yet established a small group in your local church or community, feel free to adapt this overview to fit your own group's needs.

Theology, Vision, Structure of Small Groups
Theology of Small Groups (Why Are We Doing This?)

- God is an eternal community of Father, Son, and Holy Spirit, and He made us in His image (Genesis 1:26). We were designed to live life in community.

- The command to love God is joined with the command to love others (Matthew 22:37-40). That means we will experience more of God when we experience community with others.

- Our church, communities, and world need this. Christian witness is only as powerful as the love demonstrated in community with one another. "By this all men will know that you are My disciples, if you have love for one another" (John 13:35). Small groups help us demonstrate this kind of love to the outside world as we connect in community with one another, grow spiritually together, and serve our church, community, and world together.

The Vision for Small Groups

- To progressively develop small-group opportunities for the purpose of intentional biblical application in a relational context of accountability and connectivity.

- To have a means of measurably identifying the spiritual growth of fellow Christians.

- To develop an ongoing unified group of well-trained facilitators who will help create and maintain a relational environment for discipleship to occur.

Small-Group Values

- *Connect.* In a small group, we are connected in community by fellowshipping with one another and providing care for each other so that no one stands alone (fellowship).

- *Grow.* In a small group, we grow together by studying the curriculum and applying God's Word to our lives (education) and by responding to God's presence by praying, singing, and praising together (worship).

- *Serve.* In a small group, we serve one another by sharing leadership responsibilities, and we serve together through mission projects for our church, our community, and the world (outreach).

Small-Group Leader Expectations
Job Description

A small-group facilitator is a trained group leader who will oversee an ongoing group of no more than 12 people. The facilitator will encourage connection, growth, and service within the small group by…

> modeling an openness to share his or her faith story
> facilitating the discussion of the approved curriculum
> encouraging participation by all group members
> coordinating prayer and care for group members

Expectations

- All small-group facilitators will be growing Christians who have placed their faith in Christ alone for salvation and have a growing, personal relationship with Him. They must also be members of a local church.

- They will commit to a minimum of one year of service (two semesters).

- They will help their group connect with one another in community, grow through the discussion and application of God's Word, and promote an environment of service and care for one another.

- During each semester (fall and spring) they will

assemble their group a minimum of twice a month with one additional scheduled time of outside fellowship and one service project.

- They will commit to personally calling each group member at least once a month for encouragement and prayer.
- They will report issues, questions, and challenges that require a pastoral response to the appropriate person.

Contacting Potential Members

When contacting potential members or newly added members for the first time, it is important to be intentional. Prepare by reviewing what the small group means to its members and will hopefully mean for your new member. Small-group community life is still foreign to many newcomers. Therefore, give them an idea of what to expect in the group and answer any questions they may have. Please note that a first contact is best done over the phone.

Get to know your new group member. Share a little about your background and invite the person to do the same.

Explain your role as a facilitator (see Small-Group Leader Expectations above).

Ask the person about his or her expectation of the small-group experience. What do they hope to get out of this? You can share some of your aspirations as well.

Give them some expectations. They should expect to meet at least twice a month. Remind them that you hope all members will take ownership for the group by sharing openly and encouraging each other. Make sure they understand that each semester they will be invited to one service event and one additional small-group fellowship time.

Make Your First Meeting Great
Goals of the First Meeting

- Rekindle relationships and meet new members.
- Clarify your group's direction, expectations, and commitments.
- Briefly discuss the curriculum you will use.
- Pray that each person will build relationships and grow spiritually.

Items Needed for the First Meeting

- A meal is not necessary at every meeting but is helpful for the first meeting.
- Hand out copies of your small-group covenant (at the end of this appendix). Everyone should sign the covenant and and keep a copy.
- Nametags are particularly helpful if you have new members.

Contact Your Group in Advance

Contact your group members one week before the first meeting to welcome them to the group and inform them of the location and time of your group.

Three Essential Elements of Your Meeting
Welcome, Mingle, and Talk While You Eat

Studies show that the first seven seconds a person spends in a room can make or break the remainder of their experience in that room. Here are some tips for making your home or meeting place a welcoming environment:

- Greet each person when they arrive.

- Introduce new members to existing members.

- Never let a newcomer sit alone while waiting for the meeting to start.

- Have drinks available when people arrive.

- Play upbeat music as they arrive.

- Provide a clean home or meeting space and turn off your phone.

- Let people know when your meeting will begin in five minutes.

An Agenda for Your First Meeting

Icebreaker. Use the first five or ten minutes to help members get to know each other. If you don't have new members, try sharing things people may not know about you.

Worship and prayer. Singing worship songs is optional, but some groups find this brings them closer together. Prayer is not optional—it's an important component of your group life. There are several ways to incorporate prayer listed below.

- *Popcorn prayer.* Invite people to take turns praying as they are led to do so, and designate one person to close.

- *Groups, clusters, or prayer partners.* Divide the larger group into smaller groups and encourage them to share prayer requests and praise reports with each other.

- *Topical prayer.* As a group, choose one topic to pray about.

- *Written prayers.* Consider praying the psalms together. Take turns reading them aloud.

Covenant. This is one of the most pivotal small-group tools to set the tone for your group.

- Review the small-group covenant in detail (see the end of this appendix).

- Highlight what it means to make one's attendance at the group a priority. Remember that attendance affects the cohesiveness of the entire group.

- Think outside the box. What else does the group want to commit to? Maybe your group will also covenant to be transparent or to hold each other accountable. This is the perfect time to clarify some of the group members' expectations.

Curriculum. You have a lot of ground to cover in your first group meeting. Do not push the time schedule; rather, let the meeting have a natural flow. But for the sake of establishing a routine, take some time to highlight the curriculum you have selected. If time does not permit that you go deeper, assure the members that your normal routine will allow for more conversation and more application of the Word.

Dessert Conversation

The conversation between group members after the meeting can be just as important as conversations during the general meeting time. Use this time to get to know what people are all about. Talk about hobbies and families, and thank your members for their commitment to the group.

Small-Group Meeting Time Allocation

Each session will last between 1.75 and 2 hours. With 12 participants in each group, it is important that facilitators learn to manage their group time. Below is a typical agenda. Please note that this will not be consistent with every group meeting.

> Pre-meeting, greeting, and eating: 10 minutes
> Icebreaker: 10 minutes
> Worship and prayer: 20 minutes
> Curriculum: 60 minutes
> Wrap-up: 15 minutes

Group Attendance Policy

Groups historically experience 30 to 40 percent attrition rates. This is not an excuse for poor leadership or follow-up—attrition can happen for reasons beyond the facilitator's control.

One key way to address attrition is to take regular attendance at each meeting. This helps to communicate that attendance is important (it is one of the group values in the small-group covenant). More importantly, it reminds you as the facilitator to follow up with group members who are beginning to regularly miss your meetings.

• When you need to follow up with a group member,

make certain the conversation is about care and connection, not primarily about attendance. You are checking in to see if they need anything, catch them up on what is going on in the group, and invite them to the next meeting.

- The goal in every group is to keep a group member connected. However, if a group member has missed more than half of the scheduled group meetings in a semester (most groups meet about eight times in a semester, so four meetings are a good rule of thumb), they can be removed from your roster. Please make one final contact with your group member to let them know that they are always welcome to sign up for another group in the next semester of small groups.

Another key way of addressing attrition is to have group members share responsibilities in the group, such as coordinating snacks, facilitating one of the lessons, opening their home for a group meeting, following up on prayer, or organizing a fellowship time or service event. Whenever a group member has a role or responsibility, they will be more committed to attend.

Maintaining Confidentiality

Small groups provide a community experience that includes intentional biblical application in a relational context of accountability and connectivity. One component that helps accomplish this vision is confidentiality. Confidentiality is simply the ability to trust each other within the group. This is a vital part of the small-group covenant because it creates opportunities for everyone to discuss issues without fear that they will be shared outside the group. This level of trust means that people are free to share what is on their heart without experiencing a spirit of negative judgment. No one should share sensitive material with anyone outside the group. There are three important reasons why confidentiality is so important to the life of a small group.

Confidentiality Builds Trust

Most people aren't naturally trusting. They may have been hurt too many times in the past, so now they choose to trust no one. However, group confidentiality can help people believe in true friendship and trust again. Trust in others creates a foundation for people to ultimately trust God with their lives. Are people having a hard time opening up in your group meetings? Does all the group conversation remain on the surface? You may want to evaluate the level of trust displayed in your group. It could mean that people are just not trusting each other enough to truly tell how they feel. As their leader, when you choose to open up and share your struggles and concerns, you help to create an environment for others to be more open and transparent about their issues.

Confidentiality Encourages Confession

Confession is a much-neglected spiritual discipline. Although it is often overlooked, confession is the catalyst for spiritual victory and freedom. "It is the way we find the accountability needed to break the chains of sin in our lives" (Tom Damante). When confession becomes a regular practice within your group, the group will encounter a level of freedom in Christ that may not be experienced within a regular church service. Confession isn't always a comfortable practice at first. In fact, it can be very awkward! For instance, there may be someone in your group who has been struggling with a particular addiction for years but has never felt comfortable enough to reveal it until joining your group. A word of caution—where there is open confession, there must also be accountability. "Group confession is not a practice where people can share the dirtiness and sinfulness of their lives without ever having to change. Confession *must* be followed up by accountability so that group members will become more like Christ in that situation of their lives" (Tom Damante). "Therefore, confess your sins to one another and pray for one another, so that you may be healed" (James 5:16).

Confidentiality Protects Against Gossip

Gossip is a major problem in the church today. This is why confidentiality is so important to the life of a small group. When confidentiality becomes a priority in your group, the message will become very clear to all: What is said in our group stays in our group! When your group environment is a safe place to share, there is no need to gossip about anyone. Mutual respect for everyone is built and sustained by not talking with others outside of the group meetings about the conversations that take place in your group sessions. However, you are *not* gossipping when you include your leadership team on issues where people are hurting themselves or hurting others. Those must be communicated to your pastor. "A gossip betrays a confidence; so avoid anyone who talks too much" (Proverbs 20:19 NIV). "A gossip betrays a confidence, but a trustworthy person keeps a secret" (Proverbs 11:12-13 NIV).

Tips For Maintaining Confidentiality

1. Review the ground rules of the small-group covenant (see the end of this appendix), making sure to emphasize confidentiality.

- Briefly review the need for confidentiality before each group session.

- Review and sign the group covenant every fall and spring when a new semester begins.

- Review when a new member joins your group.

- Review when confidentiality has been violated or broken.

2. Commend the group for doing a good job maintaining confidentiality.

3. Redirect all conversations that seem to be headed toward gossip.

4. When sending electronic information or prayer requests, clearly state that all communication must remain within your group only.

5. Ask permission before publicly or socially posting photos, comments, prayer requests, and other personal information that pertains to any group member.

6. Pray and seek God's help in maintaining confidentiality in your group.

Issues to Guard Against in Small Groups

- a group member whose issue or problem is overtaking the group

- a group member who is disruptive to the life of the

group—draining its resources, using the group as a personal business network, and so on

- unhealthy relationships forming within the group
- conflict and disagreements between group members
- a group member who clearly and consistently violates Scripture, bringing shame on the name of Jesus Christ

Establishing Healthy Boundaries

Traffic lanes, stop signs, traffic lights, yield signs, walls, picket fences, and hedges all have one thing in common—they all provide boundaries. Just as these physical boundaries establish limits in our society, healthy boundaries will help establish appropriate limits in the life of the facilitator and the group.

Boundaries in Your Group

Your small group may encounter difficult situations that may be beyond the capacity of your group, such as...

emotional or mental-health issues requiring professional therapy
bitterness or hostility toward a church or its leaders
death or chronic illness
debilitating financial hardship
contentious divorce

This issues are beyond the boundaries of normal small-group life and should be referred to a pastor.

Self Boundaries

How is your relationship with your group members? Do you say yes when you want to say no? Do you take on tasks that are unreasonable or unhealthy? Do you wear yourself out trying to please others and give in to what they want without taking yourself and your family into consideration? Do you expect others to regularly meet your wants even if it inconveniences them? If your answer to any of these questions is yes, you may have unclear boundaries in your life.

People with healthy boundaries take responsibility for their own lives and allows others to live responsibly in theirs. People with healthy boundaries make sacrifices for people but only at the appropriate time and in the appropriate way. We should be available for people in crisis but unavailable to inappropriate demands. Being kind and gracious is not a blank check for your group members to continually drain you emotionally, physically, financially, and spiritually.

When we set healthy boundaries and abide by them, we exhibit self-control (Galatians 5:22-23). Boundaries are a fruit of submitting to God's will, and if we seek His guidance, He will enable us to make godly choices.

Tips to Remember about Self Boundaries

- Know your limitations (physical, financial, spiritual).

- Your family always comes before your group members.

- It is okay to say no to some requests for your time and resources.

- Speak the truth in love (Ephesians 4:15) when someone is consistently transgressing your boundaries.

- When engaging with the opposite gender, always have an additional leader present.

- Do not put yourself in potentially morally compromising situations.

- Pray for and utilize wisdom and discernment from God when faced with decisions about your time and resources. This may mean involving other godly leaders and friends to help in your decision making.

- Say yes only for the right reasons.

- Don't try to please others when making decisions.

- Don't violate other members' boundaries.

Group Covenant

The Purpose of Small Groups

Small groups provide a community experience that includes intentional biblical application in a relational context of accountability and connectivity. Group members will meet together for the purpose of connecting, growing, and serving together.

Structure

1. My group will meet _____ times a month.

2. My group will meet on
   (day of the week) _____ from
   (month) _____ through
   (month) _____.

3. The group sessions will begin at (time) _____
   and end at _____.

4. We will meet at (location)

   _____.

5. We will be studying (topic) _____
   _____.

6. We will covenant together to meet at least once per semester
   for fellowship outside of our regular group time.

7. We will also choose a service project and commit to serving
   together at least once per semester.

Values or Ground Rules

Attendance. We will make the group meeting a priority by attending all meetings and arriving on time. If we cannot attend or will run late, we will contact our group facilitator in advance of the meeting.

Participation. Our group will value the full participation of every group member. We will prepare for each meeting by studying the lesson in advance. We will listen attentively to each group member without interrupting them or carrying on separate conversations.

Confidentiality. For authentic community to form, we must be able to trust each other in the group. This means that issues discussed within the group will not be shared outside of the group.

Connectivity. Our group will value the building of relationships among group members. This means we will commit to pray for the other group members on a weekly basis, follow up on needs that are shared within the group, and seek to hold one another accountable to grow in our walk of discipleship.

Commitment. I commit to uphold the group values reflected in this group covenant.

Signature _____

Date _____

ABOUT DR. TONY EVANS

Dr. Tony Evans is founder and senior pastor of the 9500-member Oak Cliff Bible Fellowship in Dallas, founder and president of The Urban Alternative, chaplain of the NBA's Dallas Mavericks, and author of *Destiny* and *Victory in Spiritual Warfare*. His radio broadcast, *The Alternative with Dr. Tony Evans*, can be heard on more than 1000 outlets and in more than 130 countries.

THE URBAN ALTERNATIVE

Dr. Evans and The Urban Alternative (TUA) equip, empower, and unite Christians to impact *individuals, families, churches,* and *communities* to restore hope and transform lives.

We believe the core cause of the problems we face in our personal lives, homes, churches, and societies is a spiritual one. Therefore, the only way to address them is spiritually. We've tried political, social, economic, and even religious agendas. It's time for a kingdom agenda—God's visible and comprehensive rule over every area of life—because when we function as we were designed, God's divine power changes everything. It renews and restores as the life of Christ is made manifest in our own. As we align ourselves under Him, He brings about full restoration from deep within. In this atmosphere, people are revived and made whole.

As God's kingdom impacts us, it impacts others—transforming every sphere of life. When each sphere of life functions in accordance with God's Word, the outcomes are evangelism, discipleship, and community impact. As we learn how to govern ourselves under God, we transform the institutions of family, church, and society according to a biblically based kingdom perspective. Through Him, we are touching heaven and changing earth.

To achieve our goal, we use a variety of strategies, methods, and resources for reaching and equipping as many people as possible.

Broadcast Media

Hundreds of thousands of individuals experience *The Alternative with Dr. Tony Evans* through daily radio broadcasts on more than 1000 radio outlets and in more than 130 countries. The broadcast can also be seen on several television networks and online at TonyEvans.org.

Leadership Training

Kingdom Agenda Pastors (KAP) provides a viable network for like-minded pastors who embrace the kingdom agenda philosophy. Pastors have the opportunity to go deeper with Dr. Evans as they are given biblical knowledge, practical applications, and resources to impact individuals, families, churches, and communities. KAP welcomes senior and associate pastors of all churches.

Kingdom Agenda Pastors' Summit progressively develops church leaders to meet the demands of the twenty-first century while maintaining the gospel message and the strategic position of the church. The Summit introduces intensive seminars, workshops, and resources, addressing issues affecting the community, family, leadership, organizational health, and more.

Pastors' Wives Ministry, founded by Dr. Lois Evans, provides counsel, encouragement, and spiritual resources for pastors' wives as they serve with their husbands in ministry. The ministry focuses on the KAP Summit, which offers senior pastors' wives a safe place to reflect, renew, relax, and receive training in personal development, spiritual growth, and care for their emotional and physical well-being.

Community Impact

National Church Adopt-A-School Initiative (NCAASI) prepares churches across the country to impact communities by using public schools as the primary vehicle for effecting positive social change in urban youth and families. Leaders of churches, school districts, faith-based organizations, and other nonprofit organizations are equipped with the knowledge and tools to forge partnerships and build strong social-service delivery systems. This training is based on the comprehensive church-based community impact strategy conducted by Oak Cliff Bible Fellowship. It addresses such areas as economic development, education, housing, health revitalization, family renewal, and racial reconciliation. We also assist churches in tailoring the model to meet the specific needs of their communities while simultaneously addressing the spiritual and moral frame of reference.

Resource Development

We are fostering lifelong learning partnerships with the people we serve by providing a variety of published materials. We offer booklets, Bible studies, books, CDs, and DVDs to strengthen people in their walk with God and ministry to others.

For more information,
a catalog of Dr. Tony Evans's ministry resources,
and a complimentary copy of
Dr. Evans's devotional newsletter, call

(800) 800-3222

or write

The Urban Alternative
PO Box 4000
Dallas, TX 75208

or visit our website at

TonyEvans.org

Let Your Connection with Others
Deepen Your Connection with God

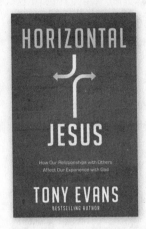

Do you want to increase your awareness of God's love for you every day?

Do you want to sense His encouragement and comfort like never before?

Dr. Tony Evans reveals that as you give these things away to others, you will personally experience them with God in a new way.

Jesus empowers His church to be His hands and feet in the world today—to share His life in your horizontal relationships. Dr. Evans demonstrates how you can become a horizontal Jesus—a channel of God's blessings to everyone around you—using several "one another" passages of Scripture, including...

Love one another
(John 13:34).

Welcome one another
(1 Peter 4:9).

Encourage one another
(Hebrews 3:13).

Forgive one another
(Colossians 3:13).

Accept one another
(Romans 15:7).

Restore one another
(Galatians 6:1-2).

As you fulfill your God-given destiny to be a conduit of God's grace, you will experience His flow of life in and through you like never before.

More Great Harvest House Books
by Dr. Tony Evans

A Moment for Your Soul

In this uplifting devotional, Dr. Evans offers a daily reading for Monday through Friday and one for the weekend—all compact, powerful, and designed to reach your deepest need. Each entry includes a relevant Scripture reading for the day.

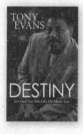

Destiny

Dr. Evans shows you the importance of finding your God-given purpose. He helps you discover and develop a custom-designed life that leads to the expansion of God's kingdom. Embracing your personal assignment from God will lead to your deepest satisfaction, God's greatest glory, and the greatest benefit to others.

The Power of God's Names

Dr. Evans shows that it's through the names of God that the nature of God is revealed. By understanding the characteristics of God as revealed through His names, you will be better equipped to face the challenges life throws at you.

Praying Through the Names of God

Dr. Evans reveals insights into some of God's powerful names and provides prayers based on those names. Your prayer life will be revitalized as you connect your needs with the relevant characteristics of His names.

Victory in Spiritual Warfare

Dr. Evans demystifies spiritual warfare and empowers you with a life-changing truth: Every struggle faced in the physical realm has its root in the spiritual realm. With passion and practicality, Dr. Evans shows you how to live a transformed life in and through the power of Christ's victory.

30 Days to Overcoming Emotional Strongholds

Dr. Evans identifies the most common and problematic emotional strongholds and demonstrates how you can break free from them—by aligning your thoughts with God's truth in the Bible.

30 Days to Victory Through Forgiveness

Has someone betrayed you? Are you suffering the consequences of your own poor choices? Or do you find yourself asking God, *Why did You let this happen?* Like a skilled physician, Dr. Tony Evans leads you through a step-by-step remedy that will bring healing to that festering wound and get you back on your journey to your personal destiny.

To learn more about Harvest House books and
to read sample chapters, visit our website:

www.harvesthousepublishers.com

HARVEST HOUSE PUBLISHERS
EUGENE, OREGON